Buddy Ran Away

by Thea Feldman
illustrated by Tom LaBaff

Scott Foresman
is an imprint of

PEARSON

Glenview, Illinois • Boston, Massachusetts • Chandler, Arizona
Upper Saddle River, New Jersey

Every effort has been made to secure permission and provide appropriate credit for photographic material. The publisher deeply regrets any omission and pledges to correct errors called to its attention in subsequent editions.

Unless otherwise acknowledged, all photographs are the property of Pearson.

Photo locations denoted as follows: Top (T), Center (C), Bottom (B), Left (L), Right (R), Background (Bkgd)

Illustrations by Tom LaBaff

Photograph 16 Corbis

ISBN 13: 978-0-328-51411-3
ISBN 10:   0-328-51411-X

10 11 12 13   V0FL 17 16 15 14

"I can't believe the weekend is over already," Sam said. "Thanks for inviting Buddy and me up to your cabin. We had a great time!"

"I did too. I can't believe my parents are packing the car to go home already," said Alan. "It was fun having you here. And Buddy never ran out of things to sniff!"

Buddy yipped and went back to sniffing the ground.

Suddenly, the reeds by the bank of the mountain stream made a whooshing sound. A rabbit bounded out and scampered right in front of the boys!

"Wow!" Alan exclaimed. "That rabbit ran by so fast! I almost missed it!"

"It must have been taking a drink in that gully next to the stream," Sam said. "We probably startled it."

Buddy had seen the rabbit too. His yips changed to a loud bark. The rabbit disappeared into the tall grass, and Buddy ran after it. His tail wagged excitedly.

"Wait, boy! Buddy, come back!" Sam shouted. But the dog didn't return. The boys could not see him anywhere. Sam ran after Buddy, and Alan headed back to the cabin to get his dad.

"Buddy!" Sam called over and over. "Buddy! Come back, boy! It's time to go home!" But the only thing Sam heard was his own voice as it echoed off the mountain.

Alan and Mr. Hall made their way through the tall grass. They caught up with Sam at the edge of the mountain forest.

"Sam, it looks as though Buddy is far ahead of us," said Mr. Hall.

"Well, how do we get through this underbrush?" Sam asked. "I'm sure that Buddy is somewhere in the forest!"

"The brush is too thick, Sam," said Mr. Hall gently. "We'd have to be Buddy's size to move around safely in there."

"So what do we do?" Sam asked. He was trying not to panic.

"We can wait here awhile and see if Buddy comes back," said Mr. Hall.

Sam, Alan, and Mr. Hall waited for an hour. They called Buddy's name until their voices were hoarse. But the dog did not come back.

"Why would Buddy run off like that?" Alan wondered aloud as they walked back through the tall thatched grass toward the cabin.

"Well," replied Mr. Hall, "Buddy is a beagle. He's doing what beagles do. They like to chase things."

"But why didn't he come back?" Sam pleaded. "Something must have happened to him!"

"Sam, we don't know that. Buddy is probably a little turned around. He hasn't been up in the mountain forest before."

"That's right," Sam said.

"I'm sorry, Sam, but when we get back to the cabin, it will be time to head home. We have a long drive back to the valley."

"I can't leave Buddy up here alone!" Sam said. He couldn't face the thought of leaving his best friend behind.

"Here's what we'll do," said Mr. Hall. "We'll post a sign about Buddy at the cabin rental office. Buddy has tags on his collar with his name and your phone number. I'm sure someone will find him in a day or two and give you a call."

On the way home Sam threw a few small pieces of his clothing out the car window. His idea was that Buddy would find them and pick up his scent. Then his dog could follow the scent home.

Sam watched for Buddy all the way down the mountain road. But he didn't see any dogs at all.

Sam's mom gave him a big hug when he got home. After he told her about Buddy, she hugged him again.

"If we don't hear anything by the weekend, we'll go and look for him again," Mom promised.

The days and nights were long for Sam. He missed taking his dog for walks and playing with him after school. He missed having Buddy curled up at his feet while he did his homework. Most of all, he missed the yipping sounds Buddy made in his sleep at night.

Sam's class spent time in the school library that week, and Sam chose a book about beagles to take home. He wanted to learn everything he could about beagles and their instincts.

There was no news about Buddy that week. On the weekend, Sam and his mom traveled to the mountain cabins. Mr. Hall and Alan went along too. But they didn't find Buddy.

Sam stayed hopeful, but he was sad. He didn't want to play with his friends. He didn't even want pizza, his favorite food. All he wanted was Buddy.

Sam's mother offered to get him another dog, but Sam wasn't interested. He read in his library book that beagles are born with the instinct to hunt. He learned that beagles are experts at finding and following a scent. Sam knew that leaving that scent trail had been a wise thing to do. He was not ready to give up on Buddy.

Another long week went by. Sam woke up on Saturday morning to the sound of barking. The bark sounded just like Buddy's! Sam ran to his front door and pulled it open. He could not believe his eyes! There was Buddy, sitting on the welcome mat. He was wagging his tail harder than ever!

Sam was so surprised! "Good boy! You followed the scent trail!" he cried happily. Sam knelt down, and Buddy scrambled into his arms. Sam clutched his dog tightly. "Welcome home, Buddy! Welcome home!"

Animal Instincts

There have been many cases of dogs traveling long distances to get back to their owners. They use their instincts, or behaviors they are born with. Instincts do not need to be taught.

Hounds, like beagles, love to chase other animals, such as rabbits. Following a scent trail is a natural instinct for hounds.

All dogs use their noses to make sense of the world around them. Do you know any dogs? Maybe you have a dog of your own. Watch a dog for an hour. Does the dog use its sense of smell more than its other senses? Try to find out!

Beagles using their noses to investigate